JAZZ PIANO STUD... 2

John Kember

CONTENTS

© 1995 by Faber Music Ltd
This edition © 2005 by Faber Music Ltd
3 Queen Square London WC1N 3AU
Cover illustration by Vikki Liogier
Music processed by Christopher Hinkins
Printed in England by Caligraving Ltd
All rights reserved

ISBN 0-571-52450-8

TRIADS MUSIC CENTER

Glens Falls, NY 12801
518-793-2848

Introduction

Jazz relies heavily on recognisable, repeated harmonic patterns (chord sequences and/or bass lines) combined with inventive melodic and rhythmic improvisation – rather like the classical Theme and Variations.

Level 2 of *Jazz Piano Studies* sets out to explore these and other features of jazz piano styles, while aiming to develop familiarity with chords, increased independence of the hands, and a substantial repertoire of rhythmic and melodic ideas, figures and devices.

Sustain pedal
Although you will need to use the sustain pedal in the slower, more legato studies, its use should be light and limited.

Dynamics
The dynamics given are only a guide: you can choose to follow them or not as you wish.

Note on 'swing' rhythm
In this book, pieces to be played with a 'swing' feel are indicated:

In all other cases, quavers/eighth notes should be played straight.

1. WALKING BASS

Walking bass line: single notes in strict time and at a brisk, driving tempo. A strong chord progression is implied, providing a constant pulse as a background for syncopation, and leaving the right hand free for melody or chords.

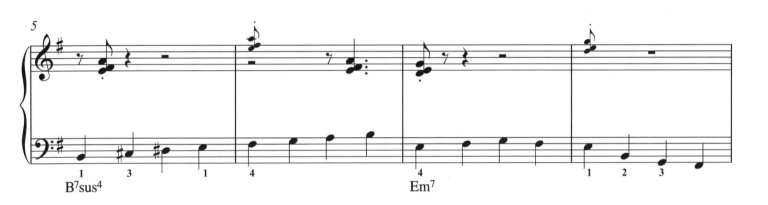

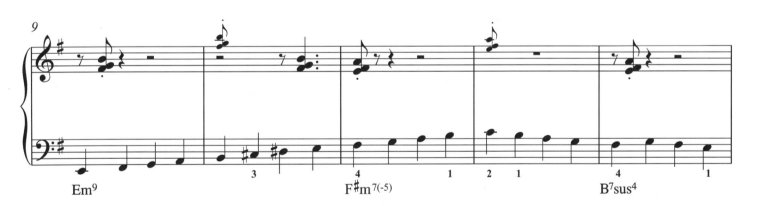

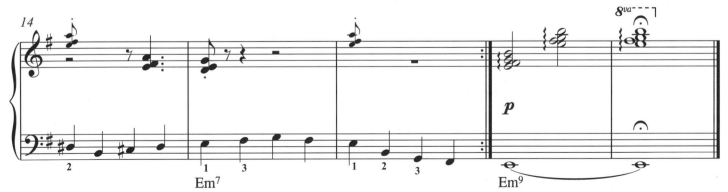

* Optional, or 2nd time only

4

2. DREAM LINES

The use of big stretches in the left hand is part of jazz history. For smaller hands however, the 7th is more comfortable. A strong chord shape can consist of just the root and 7th, or with an added fifth. This shape is particularly useful in chromatic sequences and has the advantage of giving total freedom to the right hand.

3. SOMETHING BLUE

In addition to giving the left hand both the chords and the bass line, the right hand, while playing mainly triplet figures, contains some chromatic elements and 'blue' notes.

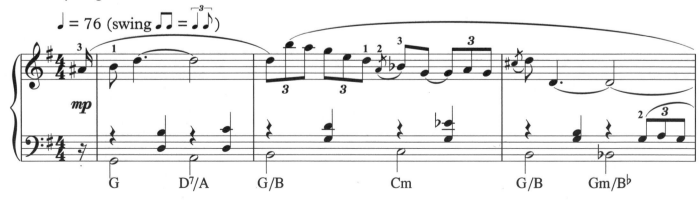

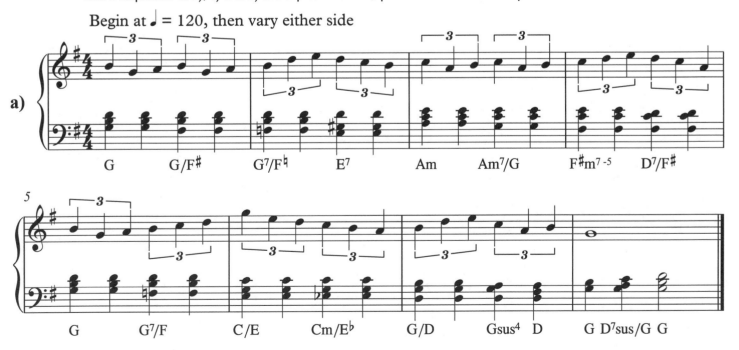

4. EXERCISES IN THREES AGAINST TWOS

Exercise a) is in playing triplet crotchets/quarter notes against a steady left hand '4-in-the-bar/measure' chord sequence. In b), c) and d) the triplet crotchets/quarter notes occur in all parts other than the bass.

Begin at ♩ = 120, then vary either side

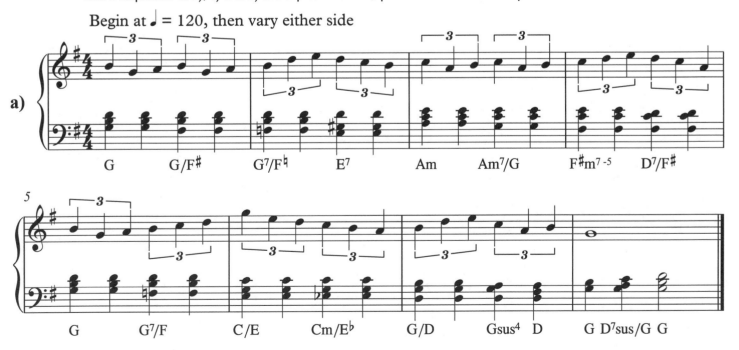

6

5. CHIEFLY CHROMATIC

A regular and characteristic feature is the use of chromatic phrasing in both single-note-style extemporised lines and chordal progressions.

8

6. RAGS TO RICHES

Needs to be bright in tone and tempo, with clear and precise rhythms and a mood of fun. The right hand counter melody in bars/measures 17–28 may be left out.

* Upper part may be omitted

7. RENDEZVOUS

A legato and expressively-shaped 'cantabile' melody, supported by a light, crisp jazz waltz rhythm. Aim for a quick tempo with almost a one-in-the-bar/measure feel.

8. FOURTH TIME LUCKY

Slower, blues style, making use of the fourth interval and right-hand octaves.

9. SIXES AND SEVENTHS

Rhythm and melody are formed from syncopated sixths for most of the piece, while the chords are largely sevenths.

10. PLAYTIME

A play on the time patterns employed. All accents and staccatos need to be crisp and precise, within a strict tempo. Keep the walking bass (middle 16 bars/measures) smooth and quiet.

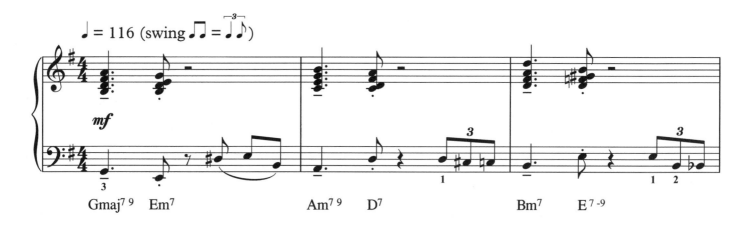

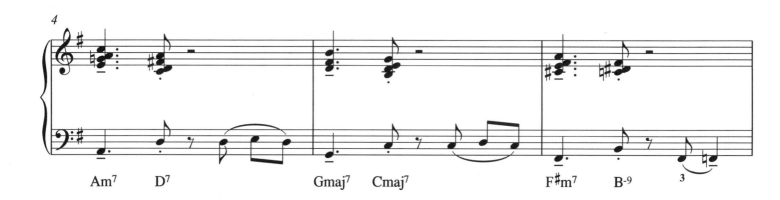

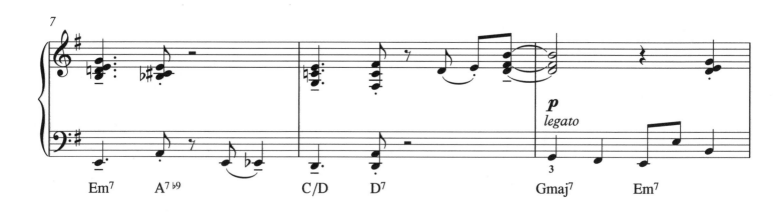

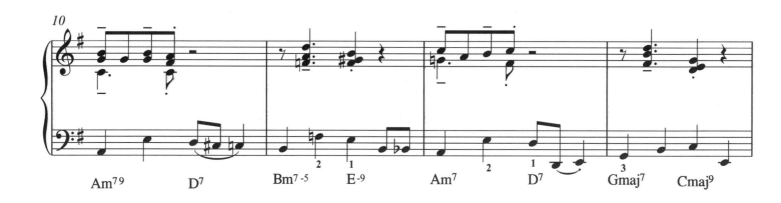

11. ROUGH BLUES

Heavy, earthy and vigorous throughout. Needs strong accents, and a positive touch and tempo.

12. SOUL MATES

The chord basis, given at the start, reflects the gospel roots in many jazz progressions. By delaying or anticipating a chord change the rhythmic character can be transformed, thereby establishing the style. Seven melodic developments occur before the chord sequence brings the piece to a close. You can play these variations in any order, leave some out, or substitute your own if you wish.

13. INTO THE BLUE

Two features are explored here: the crisp rhythmic patterns in the opening and closing sections:

and the dependence on the left hand for the chord sequence. The middle variations are based on a four-bar/measure sequence which is repeated five times.

14. REFLECTIONS

A slower, more relaxed treatment of swung quavers/eighth notes, with variations that include use of spread crotchets/quarter notes. The ending is slower and more reflective.

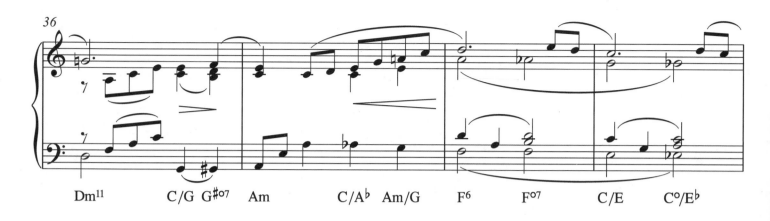

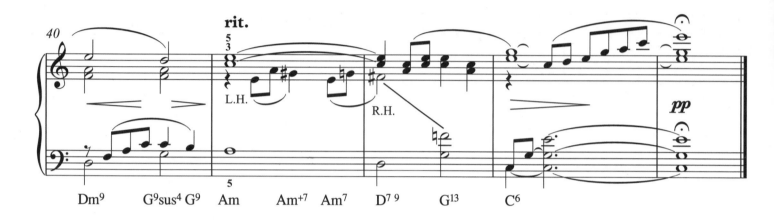

15. BRIGHT AND BREEZY

A lively $\frac{5}{4}$ time with a $\frac{3}{4}$ jazz waltz middle section.

16. RIFF-RAFF

Built on a bass riff and strong off-beat accents. The 3rd beat is anticipated throughout.

JAZZ PIANO PLUS ONE

14 original jazz pieces for piano with optional teacher part

John Kember

A great new collection of original jazz pieces, with a difference! Though the pieces work well as solos, the optional bass or top part for the teacher or a friend adds an extra dimension, whilst maintaining a constant, driving beat.

Covering a range of styles – including swing, rock, latin, ballad and blues – the 14 pieces introduce 'rootless' chords and a variety of 'comping' styles, encourage independence of the hands, and the beginnings of improvisation. So whether you are working towards a jazz exam or simply playing for fun, *Jazz Piano Plus One* is the ideal route to stylish jazz piano playing!

For players of approximately ABRSM Grade 3–5 and above.

1.   Saturday night
2.   Rhythmic rumba
3.   Straight talking
4.   Ballad
5.   Having a stomp
6.   Rootless chords
7.   Chillin' out
8.   Lucy's blues
9.   Past midnight
10. Left hand comping
11. Take it away
12. Out for the count
13. Out and about
14. Walk that bass!

FABER *ff* MUSIC